SUMMER OLYMPIC LEGENDS

VOLLEYBALL

BY NATE LeBOUTILLIER

CREATIVE ᴄ EDUCATION

CONTENTS

INTRODUCTION

Throughout human history, people have always sought to challenge themselves, to compete against others, and to discover the limits of their capabilities. Such desires can turn destructive, leading to war. But the ancient Greeks also recognized the good in these human traits, and it was because of them that the Olympic Games—featuring running races, jumping contests, throwing competitions, and wrestling and boxing matches—began more than 2,700 years ago. The ancient Olympics ended in A.D. 393, but the Games were revived in 1896 in hopes of promoting world peace through sports. Fittingly, the first "modern" Olympics were held in Athens, Greece, but they moved around the world every four years after that. In 2009, it was announced that the Games would be held in South America for the first time, going to Rio de Janeiro, Brazil, in 2016.

Every 1896 Olympian received a medal reading "International Olympic Games, Athens 1896"

In 1895, volleyball was invented in Holyoke, Massachusetts, by William G. Morgan, a YMCA physical education instructor. It did not take long for the sport—a fast-paced game involving powerful ball striking, agile defense, and tight-knit teamwork—to grow in popularity throughout the United States. In the first quarter of the 20th century, the game gained international interest as well, especially in Brazil, China, Japan, the Philippines, Poland, and Russia. Teenage athletes played volleyball as a demonstration event at the Olympic Games of 1924, but it wasn't until 1964, in Tokyo, Japan, that volleyball was introduced as an official Olympic sport.

Played at the Olympic level by both men and women, volleyball was first dominated by teams from Japan, with squads from the Soviet Union and the U.S. soon rising to capture their own shares of glory. In recent years, the sport has ascended to new levels of popularity due largely to beach volleyball, a modified form that gained Olympic status in 1996. While stars such as the Soviet Union's Yuri Chesnokov and Cuba's Regla Torres did their countries proud on indoor courts, volleyball standouts such as Americans Karch Kiraly and Kerri Walsh have made history under the sun. Whether it is played on an indoor surface or sand, or in teams of six or two, the high-leaping, ball-smashing game of volleyball has earned a place as one of the Olympics' most thrilling competitions.

ATHENS, GREECE	PARIS, FRANCE	ST. LOUIS, MISSOURI	LONDON, ENGLAND	STOCKHOLM, SWEDEN	ANTWERP, BELGIUM	PARIS, FRANCE	AMSTERDAM, NETHERLANDS	LOS ANGELES, CALIFORNIA	BERLIN, GERMANY	LONDON, ENGLAND	HELSINKI, FINLAND	MELBOURNE, AUSTRALIA	ROME, ITALY	TOKYO, JAPAN	MEXICO CITY, MEXICO	MUNICH, WEST GERMANY	MONTREAL, QUEBEC	MOSCOW, SOVIET UNION	LOS ANGELES, CALIFORNIA	SEOUL, SOUTH KOREA	BARCELONA, SPAIN	ATLANTA, GEORGIA	SYDNEY, AUSTRALIA	ATHENS, GREECE	BEIJING, CHINA	LONDON, ENGLAND
1896	1900	1904	1908	1912	1920	1924	1928	1932	1936	1948	1952	1956	1960	1964	1968	1972	1976	1980	1984	1988	1992	1996	2000	2004	2008	2012

A PIONEER AND PILLAR

YURI CHESNOKOV SOVIET UNION

OLYMPIC COMPETITIONS: 1964 (AS PLAYER); 1972, 1976 (AS COACH)

Although he was a fierce **hitter** and tough **blocker** while playing for the Soviet Union in the 1964 Olympics in Tokyo, the best part of Yuri Chesnokov's game was his mind. With a gift for strategy that would later become fully evident in his efforts as a coach, Chesnokov led the Soviets to an 8–1 record in **round-robin** play at the Tokyo Games, good for the first-ever gold medal in men's Olympic volleyball. Chesnokov had honed his game playing for the Central Army Sports Club (CSKA) in Moscow. Two years after the 1964 Olympics, he retired as a player and became coach of the CSKA team, which was the top club in the country. In 1970, he was handed the reins to the national team as well.

At the 1972 Olympics, held in Munich, West Germany, expectations for the Soviet men's volleyball team were high. The Soviets had won their second consecutive Olympic gold in the 1968

A Romanian stamp celebrating volleyball and its inaugural Olympic tournament in the 1964 Games

Games in Mexico City and appeared to be on the verge of a **dynasty** with a style that was both hard-hitting and tactically supreme. In Munich, Chesnokov coached his team to a perfect 5–0 record in **pool play**, only to watch as East Germany pulled off a major upset by upending his squad in four **sets**. Although the Soviets recovered from the startling loss with an easy, three-set victory over Bulgaria in the bronze-medal match, their overall performance was considered a failure by officials within the "Soviet Sports Machine"—the nationalistic sports program that produced many successful Olympic athletes in numerous sports in the 1970s.

The 1976 Olympics, held in Montreal, Quebec, gave Chesnokov and the Soviet team a chance to redeem themselves. Again, the Soviets were dominant in pool play, losing no sets in their three **preliminary** matches. In the semifinals, they ousted Cuba with another perfect, three-set win before facing upstart Poland in the gold-medal match. In one of the great Olympic volleyball finales in history, the Soviets roared out to a two-sets-to-none lead, only to fall victim to a Polish rally led by

Poland's top star, Ed Skorek, who seemed to be everywhere. No advice Chesnokov could impart could save his players from falling in the final three sets as Poland won the gold.

Soon after the 1976 Olympics, Chesnokov retired from coaching and took a leadership position in the International Volleyball Federation (FIVB). From 1978 through 1998, Chesnokov held various posts in the FIVB, attending every Olympiad to promote the sport of volleyball. When Chesnokov passed away in 2010, Jizhong Wei, president of the FIVB, said of him, "He was a pillar of the FIVB who made an enormous contribution to international volleyball. He had a tremendous work ethic and touched many lives within the international volleyball community. He was not only a legend of Russian volleyball, but internationally, he was one of the most respected persons within our sport, as a player, manager, coach, and an administrator."

> **"He had a tremendous work ethic and touched many lives within the international volleyball community."**
>
> – Jizhong Wei

ATHENS, GREECE	PARIS, FRANCE	ST. LOUIS, MISSOURI	LONDON, ENGLAND	STOCKHOLM, SWEDEN	ANTWERP, BELGIUM	PARIS, FRANCE	AMSTERDAM, NETHERLANDS	LOS ANGELES, CALIFORNIA	BERLIN, GERMANY	LONDON, ENGLAND	HELSINKI, FINLAND	MELBOURNE, AUSTRALIA	ROME, ITALY	TOKYO, JAPAN	MEXICO CITY, MEXICO	MUNICH, WEST GERMANY	MONTREAL, QUEBEC	MOSCOW, SOVIET UNION	LOS ANGELES, CALIFORNIA	SEOUL, SOUTH KOREA	BARCELONA, SPAIN	ATLANTA, GEORGIA	SYDNEY, AUSTRALIA	ATHENS, GREECE	BEIJING, CHINA	LONDON, ENGLAND
1896	1900	1904	1908	1912	1920	1924	1928	1932	1936	1948	1952	1956	1960	1964	1968	1972	1976	1980	1984	1988	1992	1996	2000	2004	2008	2012

JAPAN'S HARD-WON MEDALS

1964 TOKYO, JAPAN

In 1964, just prior to the Olympic Games that were to be held in Tokyo, a reporter for *Sports Illustrated* named Eric Whitehead wrote an influential article that would affect the world of volleyball. Whitehead had gained access to the Dai Nippon textile mill in Kaizuka near Osaka,

Japanese star Masae Kasai and her teammates receive their gold medals during the Tokyo Games

8

Japan, the place where the Japanese women's volleyball team both trained and worked. In a groundbreaking piece of journalism, Whitehead skewered Hirofumi Daimatsu, a worker at Dai Nippon and the team's coach, for what he called cruel and inhumane treatment of the women on the team. The women reportedly worked in the mill from 8:00 A.M. to 3:30 P.M. and then practiced volleyball from 4:00 P.M. until midnight or even into the early morning hours. In the practices, Hirofumi would belittle the players as they repeatedly dove to the floor to **dig** volleyballs, and many of the players would be sobbing with exhaustion, pain, or embarrassment by practice's end. "I was growing my nails, because I wanted to retain some of my femininity," said Masae Kasai, the team's captain and best player, years later. "[Hirofumi] thought I was growing my nails to hurt him, which wasn't true, but I did often wish the ball would hit him in the face."

Japan's drive for Olympic glory in 1964 meant pain and exhaustion for such players as Kinuko Tanida

Despite the suffering of the Japanese players, the team performed exceedingly well at the 1964 Olympics, the Games at which volleyball debuted. Japanese spectators, already in love with the sport of volleyball, flocked to see both its women's and men's teams play. While the men's team finished with a 7–2 record and the bronze medal, it was the only team in the 10-nation tournament to defeat the gold-medal-winning Soviet Union. The Japanese women, meanwhile, were completely dominant, winning all five of their matches in a six-team tournament to easily capture gold.

The Japanese women's team had no exceedingly tall players—Kasai, at 5-foot-9, was its tallest—but they covered the court like a blanket with their sprawling dives and rolling digs. In all, they lost just a single set when Coach Hirofumi—noticing a Soviet coach taking notes from the stands—put in many of his reserves in a match against Poland in an effort to counteract this scouting. In Japan's final match, against the previously undefeated Soviets, Hirofumi's squad won 15–11, 15–8, and 15–13. For the tournament, the Japanese women outscored their opponents 238–93.

Not surprisingly, most of Japan's female players retired from volleyball following the 1964 Games. Still, Japan remained a major medal contender in the Olympics that followed. The men's team won silver in 1968 and gold in 1972. The women's team won silver in 1968 and 1972, gold again in 1976, and bronze in 1984. Hirofumi later became a member of Japanese parliament. Kasai spent time promoting volleyball and coaching—most prominently as the coach of Japan's 2004 women's Olympic team, which fell to eventual champion China.

Coach Hirofumi is hoisted aloft by his players after they claimed the sports' first Olympic gold

1896 ATHENS, GREECE
1900 PARIS, FRANCE
1904 ST. LOUIS, MISSOURI
1908 LONDON, ENGLAND
1912 STOCKHOLM, SWEDEN
1920 ANTWERP, BELGIUM
1924 PARIS, FRANCE
1928 AMSTERDAM, NETHERLANDS
1932 LOS ANGELES, CALIFORNIA
1936 BERLIN, GERMANY
1948 LONDON, ENGLAND
1952 HELSINKI, FINLAND
1956 MELBOURNE, AUSTRALIA
1960 ROME, ITALY
1964 TOKYO, JAPAN
1968 MEXICO CITY, MEXICO
1972 MUNICH, WEST GERMANY
1976 MONTREAL, QUEBEC
1980 MOSCOW, SOVIET UNION
1984 LOS ANGELES, CALIFORNIA
1988 SEOUL, SOUTH KOREA
1992 BARCELONA, SPAIN
1996 ATLANTA, GEORGIA
2000 SYDNEY, AUSTRALIA
2004 ATHENS, GREECE
2008 BEIJING, CHINA
2012 LONDON, ENGLAND

THE GREAT BOMBER

EDWARD SKOREK POLAND OLYMPIC COMPETITIONS: 1968, 1972, 1976

Born in Tomaszów Mazowiecki, Poland, some 70 miles from the capital city of Warsaw, Edward Skorek learned to play volleyball at a young age. He grew to a height of 6-foot-4 and was soon pummeling volleyballs all over courts in Poland and around the world.

The 1976 Games in Montreal (pictured) were the stage for the pinnacle moment of Edward Skorek's career

With the 24-year-old Skorek, nicknamed "The Great Bomber," leading the way, the Polish men's team went an impressive 6–3 in the 1968 Olympics yet finished out of the medals in fifth place. The 1972 Olympics were a disappointment to the Polish team, as it won just two of six games. Although team captain Skorek and his teammates returned home with no medals, they used the disappointment as fuel for improvement and intensified their training. It was then, too, that the Polish team's coach, Hubert Wagner—a player on Poland's 1968 Olympic team—added an important new element to the offense.

At the 1974 FIVB Men's World Championship, held in Mexico City, Skorek and the Poles unveiled a new system that featured a backrow attack. In this system, which required great teamwork and quick thinking, a hitter, most often Skorek, called a play based on the defense's alignment as the ball was in the air between the **serve** receiver and the **setter**. Often, the Poles—and again, usually Skorek—would intentionally **spike** the ball from behind the 10-foot line, making it extremely difficult for the defense to formulate a block at the net. The system worked so well that Poland won the 1974 World Championship.

Prior to the 1976 Olympics in Montreal, Poland trained furiously. "In those days, matches of volleyball could last more than three hours," said Skorek. "So our coach prepared us by training about 10 hours a day at a high altitude of more than 2,000 feet in France before going to Montreal. We were really prepared for everything."

In Montreal, the Poles' high fitness level and efficient new system proved to be a winning combination as the team defeated South Korea (in five sets), Canada, Cuba (in five sets after losing the first two), and Czechoslovakia in pool play. In the medal round, Poland downed Japan, the defending Olympic champion, in a closely contested, five-set match.

Poland's opponents in the finale would be their vaunted neighbors, the Soviet Union. Parts of Poland and Russia had frequently been at war since the 1500s, and relations since World War II (1939–45) had been especially tense, with the Soviet Union maintaining considerable **communist** control over Poland until 1989.

The Soviets had not lost a single set leading up to the gold-medal match, and they pounced on Poland by winning two of the first three sets and taking a 15–14 lead in the fourth. But the Poles fended off the Soviets' **match point** and took set four with a thrilling 19–17 win before going on to seal the match—and the gold—with a 15–7 victory in the fifth set. "People in all of Europe were following that match on TV because it had political value," said Skorek. "We, the players, were friends to each other, but many people kept asking if our government had given us orders to lose, which we proved wrong."

ATHENS, GREECE	PARIS, FRANCE	ST. LOUIS, MISSOURI	LONDON, ENGLAND	STOCKHOLM, SWEDEN	ANTWERP, BELGIUM	PARIS, FRANCE	AMSTERDAM, NETHERLANDS	LOS ANGELES, CALIFORNIA	BERLIN, GERMANY	LONDON, ENGLAND	HELSINKI, FINLAND	MELBOURNE, AUSTRALIA	ROME, ITALY	TOKYO, JAPAN	MEXICO CITY, MEXICO	MUNICH, WEST GERMANY	MONTREAL, QUEBEC	MOSCOW, SOVIET UNION	LOS ANGELES, CALIFORNIA	SEOUL, SOUTH KOREA	BARCELONA, SPAIN	ATLANTA, GEORGIA	SYDNEY, AUSTRALIA	ATHENS, GREECE	BEIJING, CHINA	LONDON, ENGLAND
1896	1900	1904	1908	1912	1920	1924	1928	1932	1936	1948	1952	1956	1960	1964	1968	1972	1976	1980	1984	1988	1992	1996	2000	2004	2008	2012

ILLEGAL SPIKE

1976, 1980 MONTREAL, QUEBEC; MOSCOW, SOVIET UNION

In 1976, one of the smallest nations represented at the Olympics seemed to come out of nowhere to finish with 40 gold medals, the most of any country at the Games. That country was East Germany, and though its Olympic success initially brought the country glory, the shine of its medals dimmed when the world eventually found out how its success had been won.

East Germany's women's volleyball team fell from grace after its medal-winning triumph in 1980

After World War II—which canceled out the Olympiads of 1940 and 1944—the defeated nation of Germany was split into two states: West Germany and East Germany. While West Germany was aligned with the United States and **democratic** ideals, East Germany was aligned with the Soviet Union and controlled by the Stasi, the national security service responsible for reinforcing a communist system of government. In an attempt to enhance their reputation, East German leaders began to hype the value and glory of sports, especially Olympic sports. Public sports demonstrations and festivals were common, and new schools for intensive sports training cropped up, quickly welcoming talented young athletes who showed promise in certain athletic fields. Katharina Bullin, a volleyball player from East Germany, attended one such school. But what she didn't know was that the East German Sports Performance Committee and certain state leaders had decided that they would administer **steroids** to young East German athletes. "Drips, injections, pills—it was all normal, nothing strange about it," said Bullin. "And I wouldn't have known what to ask because I wasn't skeptical at all."

> **When the Soviet Union crumbled in 1991, West Germany and East Germany were reunited into a single nation for the first time in 41 years.**

A stamp showing East German athletes in a heroic pose (above); East German volleyball players (opposite)

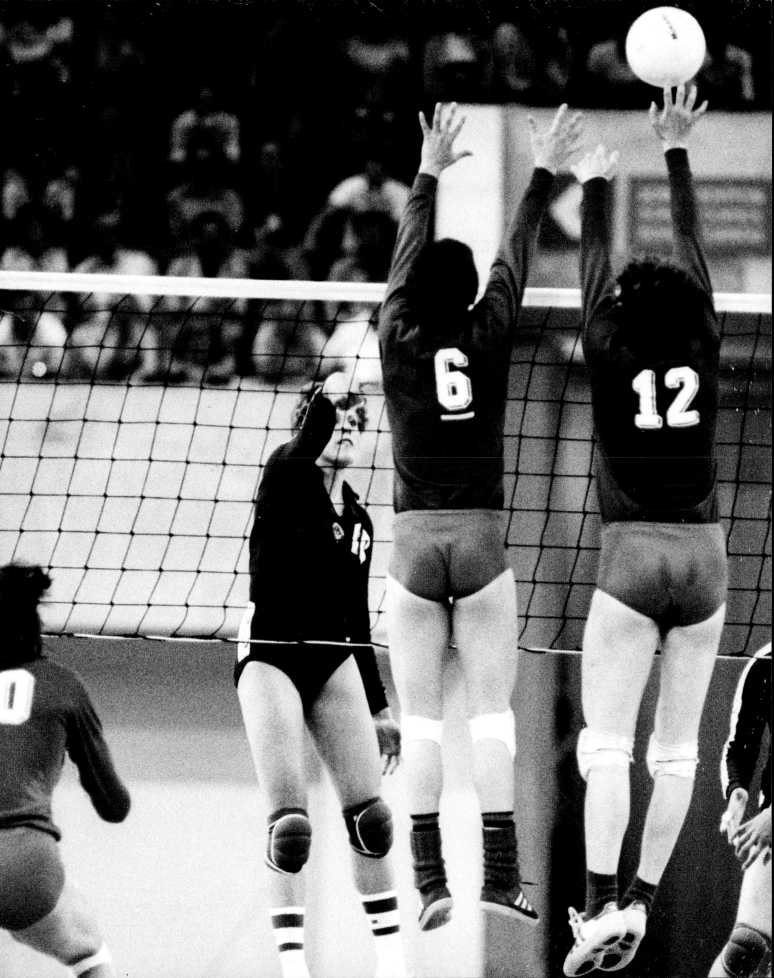

The main drug East German officials used was called Oral Turinabol, or OT, which was derived from testosterone, a hormone that occurs naturally in humans but is produced at a rate 10 times higher in males than females, making females much more sensitive to the drug. OT increased muscle and bone mass and shortened recovery time so athletes could train harder and longer, but it also generated body hair growth and increased the risk of birth defects in children born to athletes who used the steroid. It could also lead to organ and tissue breakdowns within the body, especially at the joints.

East Germany finished sixth in women's volleyball at the 1976 Olympics. In the 1980 Games in Moscow, Bullin and her East German teammates defeated Cuba and Peru. In the gold-medal match, East Germany split the first two sets with the Soviet Union before losing the final two sets, 15–13 and 15–7. Still, the silver medal represented the first (and, as of 2012, only) volleyball medal won by a women's team from Germany.

After the 1980 Games, Bullin retired from volleyball due to injuries. "Suddenly, we were growing beards, and things got really bad after the Olympics," she later explained. "I became really aggressive, probably because we weren't being doped anymore. Now I know that this was also a withdrawal symptom." In 2008, Bullin reported having had 13 surgeries as a result of worn-out joints. She was able to walk only with great effort, and she struggled with her sexual identity.

ATHENS, GREECE 1896
PARIS, FRANCE 1900
ST. LOUIS, MISSOURI 1904
LONDON, ENGLAND 1908
STOCKHOLM, SWEDEN 1912
ANTWERP, BELGIUM 1920
PARIS, FRANCE 1924
AMSTERDAM, NETHERLANDS 1928
LOS ANGELES, CALIFORNIA 1932
BERLIN, GERMANY 1936
LONDON, ENGLAND 1948
HELSINKI, FINLAND 1952
MELBOURNE, AUSTRALIA 1956
ROME, ITALY 1960
TOKYO, JAPAN 1964
MEXICO CITY, MEXICO 1968
MUNICH, WEST GERMANY 1972
MONTREAL, QUEBEC 1976
MOSCOW, SOVIET UNION 1980
LOS ANGELES, CALIFORNIA 1984
SEOUL, SOUTH KOREA 1988
BARCELONA, SPAIN 1992
ATLANTA, GEORGIA 1996
SYDNEY, AUSTRALIA 2000
ATHENS, GREECE 2004
BEIJING, CHINA 2008
LONDON, ENGLAND 2012

KING KARCH

KARCH KIRALY U.S. OLYMPIC COMPETITIONS: 1984, 1988, 1996

With Los Angeles hosting the Olympic Games in 1984, the U.S. men's volleyball team was hoping to represent its country well and win Olympic gold for the first time. Thanks to a strong collection of players—and thanks especially to a star named Karch Kiraly—the U.S. was able to pull off the feat.

The son of Hungarian immigrants, Kiraly—whose family name means "king"—began playing

As a pioneer of the sport and a decorated champion, Karch Kiraly became the face of beach volleyball

volleyball at age six on the beaches of California with his father, Laszlo. By age 11, Karch had begun entering two-man beach volleyball tournaments with his father as his teammate. "I pushed him very hard in those days," Laszlo later acknowledged. "I was critical of him. I could see him seething inside. I forgot that he was 11 or 12 years old." Although Laszlo's training was sometimes overbearing, his work with Karch paid off when the younger Kiraly earned a scholarship to play volleyball at the University of California, Los Angeles (UCLA). Kiraly's college career was a smashing success; in four years, he contributed to three national volleyball titles and a 124–5 cumulative record. In the classroom, meanwhile, he earned a degree with honors in biochemistry.

Kiraly's two-man beach volleyball experience with his father helped him develop more than just his intensity. It helped him become a better all-around player by improving his serving, passing, setting, and blocking skills—not just hitting, which was Kiraly's forte, thanks largely to his phenomenal vertical jump, which topped 40 inches. The U.S. team of 1984 employed a "two-man" or "swing hitter" offense—in which the hitter **bumps** to the setter and is then set up for the **kill**—similar to that which Kiraly played

at UCLA. Kiraly's fine play spearheaded an American attack that earned Olympic gold in 1984. Kiraly's efforts at the 1988 Games were even more impressive. Paired with such teammates as highflyer Steve Timmons, Kiraly led the U.S. to a sound victory over the Soviet Union and earned a second volleyball gold.

Considering how long Kiraly's career ended up being, it's something of a mystery as to why he opted out of playing in the 1992 Olympics in Barcelona, when he would have been 31 years old—in his prime as a volleyball player. But part of the reason was likely that Kiraly had switched back to playing beach volleyball, a purer and more basic form of the sport that was his first love. When beach volleyball was added as an official Olympic sport in 1996, Kiraly couldn't resist returning to the Olympic stage, and along with partner Kent Steffes, he captured the inaugural gold medal in men's beach volleyball. Kiraly's playing career continued into his 40s before he finally retired to promote the beach volleyball professional tour. "Karch inspired his partners, his opponents, and the world of volleyball players to be better than they were, to be great," said Mike Dodd, a longtime beach opponent. "In the end, who could do more for a sport than that?"

Professionally, Kiraly earned many honors, including the 2002 "Best Defensive Player" award

ATHENS, GREECE	PARIS, FRANCE	ST. LOUIS, MISSOURI	LONDON, ENGLAND	STOCKHOLM, SWEDEN	ANTWERP, BELGIUM	PARIS, FRANCE	AMSTERDAM, NETHERLANDS	LOS ANGELES, CALIFORNIA	BERLIN, GERMANY	LONDON, ENGLAND	HELSINKI, FINLAND	MELBOURNE, AUSTRALIA	ROME, ITALY	TOKYO, JAPAN	MEXICO CITY, MEXICO	MUNICH, WEST GERMANY	MONTREAL, QUEBEC	MOSCOW, SOVIET UNION	LOS ANGELES, CALIFORNIA	**SEOUL, SOUTH KOREA**	BARCELONA, SPAIN	ATLANTA, GEORGIA	SYDNEY, AUSTRALIA	ATHENS, GREECE	BEIJING, CHINA	LONDON, ENGLAND
1896	1900	1904	1908	1912	1920	1924	1928	1932	1936	1948	1952	1956	1960	1964	1968	1972	1976	1980	1984	**1988**	1992	1996	2000	2004	2008	2012

PERU'S SILVER LINING

1988 SEOUL, SOUTH KOREA

Throughout the 1900s in Peru, soccer was king. But late in the century, women's volleyball gave soccer a run for its money in the hearts of Peruvians. By the 1970s, the volleyball boom had hit Peru's capital of Lima, and many impoverished children and young adults from **slums** were playing the simple game (with simple equipment) in the streets or in semi-organized clubs. "Potentially

Children practice their bumping skills while playing volleyball in the streets of Peru in 2011

good players grow like weeds," said Jesus Paniagua, a volleyball club sponsor and former member of the Federación Peruana de Voleibol, Peru's main volleyball organization. "The girls play because it is almost instinctive."

One such player was Cecilia Tait, who was discovered as a 12-year-old playing volleyball in a sandlot in one of Lima's many **shantytowns**. Tait was integrated into a bigger club and was soon playing for Peru's national junior team. In 1980, an 18-year-old Tait made the Peruvian Olympic volleyball team that competed in Moscow and finished in sixth place. Tait was joined by other talented young players on the 1984 Peruvian Olympic team that finished fourth.

By 1988, Peru's women's Olympic volleyball team had fully matured. Tait, a powerful, 6-foot left-handed spiker, had earned the nickname "The Golden Lefty." Gaby Perez, a 6-foot-4 middle blocker, anchored the defense at the net. Rosa Garcia was the setter, and she was joined by feisty yet undersized hitters and diggers Gina Torrealva, Natalia Malaga, Denise Fajardo, and Cenaida Uribe, among others. This team made its way through the tournament in Seoul, South Korea, in heart-stopping fashion, winning five-set comeback matches against China, the U.S., and Japan.

In the gold-medal match, Peru faced the Soviet Union, volleyball medalists in every previous Olympics in which it had participated. Peru shocked the Soviets by winning the first two sets, 15–10 and 15–12. With most of Peru watching on TV in the early morning hours, the Peruvians then shot out to a 12–7 lead in the third game and found themselves just three points away from Olympic gold—a gold that would have been just the second earned by any Peruvian athlete or team since marksman Edwin Vasquez Cam had earned the country's only previous gold with a winning effort in the free pistol shooting competition of 1948.

Unfortunately for Peru, the Soviets fought back to eke out a 15–13 win and then took the fourth game, 15–7, to even the match. The fifth game was possibly the tensest and most closely contested in volleyball history, with the Soviets failing to win the gold with a match point at 14–13, and then the Peruvians failing on three match-point opportunities with the score 15–14 in their favor. In the end, the Soviets prevailed, 17–15, to win the gold. But the silver medalists enjoyed fame and lasting popularity following the Olympics. In the 2000s, three of the Peruvian volleyball stars—Tait, Perez, and Uribe—were elected to the Peruvian congress.

ATHENS, GREECE
PARIS, FRANCE
ST. LOUIS, MISSOURI
LONDON, ENGLAND
STOCKHOLM, SWEDEN
ANTWERP, BELGIUM
PARIS, FRANCE
AMSTERDAM, NETHERLANDS
LOS ANGELES, CALIFORNIA
BERLIN, GERMANY
LONDON, ENGLAND
HELSINKI, FINLAND
MELBOURNE, AUSTRALIA
ROME, ITALY
TOKYO, JAPAN
MEXICO CITY, MEXICO
MUNICH, WEST GERMANY
MONTREAL, QUEBEC
MOSCOW, SOVIET UNION
LOS ANGELES, CALIFORNIA
SEOUL, SOUTH KOREA
BARCELONA, SPAIN
ATLANTA, GEORGIA
SYDNEY, AUSTRALIA
ATHENS, GREECE
BEIJING, CHINA
LONDON, ENGLAND

1896 1900 1904 1908 1912 1920 1924 1928 1932 1936 1948 1952 1956 1960 1964 1968 1972 1976 1980 1984 **1988** 1992 1996 2000 2004 2008 2012

CLASH OF THE ARCHRIVALS

1988 SEOUL, SOUTH KOREA

At the 1988 Olympic Games in Seoul, it seemed that a true and indisputable world champion of men's volleyball would finally be crowned. The men's volleyball winners of the previous two Games, the Soviet Union and the U.S., had won Olympic gold in 1980 and 1984 respectively, without the other in attendance due to **boycotts**.

Jeff Stork helped the American men's team capture volleyball gold in 1988 and bronze in 1992

America's 1988 volleyball squad was considered the best in U.S. history and was led by hitters Karch Kiraly, a remarkably proficient all-around player, and Steve Timmons, a 6-foot-5 volleyball crusher with a red flattop haircut and an explosive vertical jump. The top setter was Jeff Stork, a wily play coordinator whose left-handed serves and occasional quick **dumps** racked up points in bunches. Other powerful hitters included 6-foot-4 Bob Ctvrtlik, 6-foot-6 Doug Partie, and the tallest member of Team USA, 6-foot-8 Craig Buck. There was no doubt that the U.S. had the momentum and experience to put it at the top of the list of contenders in 1988. The Americans had dominated the 1984 Games and then won both the 1986 World Championship and the 1987 Pan American Games. Even Soviet coach Gennadi Parchin admitted, "We used to be the teacher of the world in volleyball. Now we are the students to the U.S."

The Soviet volleyball squad of 1988 included two holdovers from its 1980 Olympic gold medal-winning team—captain Yuriy Panchenko and 6-foot-3 star Vyacheslav Zaytsev—but the heart of the team was less experienced. Rising stars Andrey Kuznetsov (22 years old), Yury Cherednik (22), Yury Sapega (23), Yaroslav Antonov, (25), and Raimonds Vilde (26) may have been raw, but they made up for it in talent. And the Soviets had some momentum of their own, having won the previous nine European Championships.

The U.S. and Soviet Union's meeting in the finals was not a foregone conclusion. In pool play, Brazil downed the Soviets in a tight match, and Argentina pushed the U.S. to the maximum five sets before the Americans earned a narrow victory. But by the end of the tournament, the finals did indeed pit the Americans against their archrivals, the Soviets.

The gold-medal match saw the Soviet Union jump out to a 14–11 lead in set one. The U.S. squad then came alive, denying the Soviets victory on

Political hostilities added to the intensity of the U.S.–Soviet Union matchup during the 1988 Olympics

10 different set-point opportunities. Finally, the Soviets prevailed, 15–13, but the Americans' fuse had been lit. Led by Stork, who surprised the Soviets again and again with his quick left-handed dumps; Timmons, who skied to seemingly impossible heights on every spike attempt; and Kiraly, whose masterful digging and hitting pulled everything together, the U.S. won the next three sets by scores of 15–10, 15–4, and 15–8 to win the gold. "I was a security guard at the 1984 Games," said Ctvrtlik, who made the 1988 team as a 25-year-old. "But I remember some people had doubts [about America's superiority] because the Soviet **bloc** teams weren't there. There was something missing. Having everybody here made this special."

Steve Timmons, Craig Buck, and Bob Ctvrtlik (from left to right) go for the block versus the Soviets

1896	1900	1904	1908	1912	1920	1924	1928	1932	1936	1948	1952	1956	1960	1964	1968	1972	1976	1980	1984	1988	**1992**	**1996**	**2000**	2004	2008	2012
ATHENS, GREECE	PARIS, FRANCE	ST. LOUIS, MISSOURI	LONDON, ENGLAND	STOCKHOLM, SWEDEN	ANTWERP, BELGIUM	PARIS, FRANCE	AMSTERDAM, NETHERLANDS	LOS ANGELES, CALIFORNIA	BERLIN, GERMANY	LONDON, ENGLAND	HELSINKI, FINLAND	MELBOURNE, AUSTRALIA	ROME, ITALY	TOKYO, JAPAN	MEXICO CITY, MEXICO	MUNICH, WEST GERMANY	MONTREAL, QUEBEC	MOSCOW, SOVIET UNION	LOS ANGELES, CALIFORNIA	SEOUL, SOUTH KOREA	**BARCELONA, SPAIN**	**ATLANTA, GEORGIA**	**SYDNEY, AUSTRALIA**	ATHENS, GREECE	BEIJING, CHINA	LONDON, ENGLAND

THE RISE OF THE CUBANS

CUBAN WOMEN'S VOLLEYBALL OLYMPIC COMPETITIONS: 1992, 1996, 2000

In 1992, a powerful force arose in women's Olympic volleyball that had seemingly come out of nowhere. But Cuba had been building a powerful volleyball program for years despite not always sending its athletes to the Olympics; the communist country boycotted both the 1984 and 1988 Olympics for political reasons. Considering what the Cuban women's volleyball team was able to

Stars Mireya Luis (right) and Regla Torres helped carry Cuba to the top of the volleyball world

achieve in a single decade—capturing gold medals in the 1992, 1996, and 2000 Games—volleyball fans were left to rightly wonder if that streak might have included five golds if Cuba had participated in 1984 and 1988.

The Cuban attack in 1992 featured the powerful hitting of 5-foot-9 Mireya Luis, 5-foot-10 Marlenis Costa, and 5-foot-11 lefty Regla Bell; the setting of 5-foot-8 Lilia Izquierdo; and the fierce defense of 6-foot-3 middle blocker Regla Torres, who was just 17 years old at the Barcelona Games. Luis was the team's leader, and to watch her was to be reminded of another standout of the 1992 Olympiad: star Michael "Air" Jordan of the American men's basketball team. Like Jordan, Luis could jump through the roof—she had an amazing 36-inch vertical—and her spikes were as bold and awe-inspiring as Jordan's dunks. Cuba blew through the 1992 tournament undefeated, though it received a scare from the U.S. in a five-set semifinals match in which it was down 9–8 in the fifth set but came back to win. In the gold-medal match, Cuba downed the Unified Team from Russia (the Soviet Union had broken apart in 1991) in four sets.

In 1996, the stars of Cuba were in their prime, and they met some formidable competition in Atlanta. Cuba slogged through pool play, winning three matches but losing to both Brazil (in straight sets) and Russia. In the **knockout round**, though, Cuba came alive, first besting the U.S. in straight sets and then upending previously undefeated Brazil in a wild, five-set match. Next, Cuba took down previously undefeated China to secure gold.

The 2000 Olympics in Sydney provided Cuba with the opportunity to become the first women's team in any sport to capture three straight gold medals. In the Cubans' way, however, was an exceptionally strong Russian team. In pool play, the Russians defeated the Cubans in a tightly contested

The Cuban women's 2000 volleyball triumph was 1 of 11 gold medals claimed by Cuba in those Games

five-setter by scores of 20–25, 25–21, 21–25, 25–12, and 15–13. Cuba then stormed through the knockout portion of the tournament, beating Croatia and Brazil to set up a rematch versus Russia. The first two games were as close as could be, with Russia eking out wins of 27–25 and 34–32. But then, in a rally that could only be summoned by experience, Cuba turned the match around, winning the next three sets, 25–19, 25–18, and 15–7, to claim its third straight gold. "We were very tense because of the pressure of winning a third gold medal," said Cuba's Torres, widely considered the best player of the 2000 tournament. "Then we relaxed and changed the way we played."

Along with boxing, women's volleyball became perhaps Cuba's strongest Olympic sport in the 1990s

ATHENS, GREECE	PARIS, FRANCE	ST. LOUIS, MISSOURI	LONDON, ENGLAND	STOCKHOLM, SWEDEN	ANTWERP, BELGIUM	PARIS, FRANCE	AMSTERDAM, NETHERLANDS	LOS ANGELES, CALIFORNIA	BERLIN, GERMANY	LONDON, ENGLAND	HELSINKI, FINLAND	MELBOURNE, AUSTRALIA	ROME, ITALY	TOKYO, JAPAN	MEXICO CITY, MEXICO	MUNICH, WEST GERMANY	MONTREAL, QUEBEC	MOSCOW, SOVIET UNION	LOS ANGELES, CALIFORNIA	SEOUL, SOUTH KOREA	BARCELONA, SPAIN	ATLANTA, GEORGIA	SYDNEY, AUSTRALIA	ATHENS, GREECE	BEIJING, CHINA	LONDON, ENGLAND
1896	1900	1904	1908	1912	1920	1924	1928	1932	1936	1948	1952	1956	1960	1964	1968	1972	1976	1980	1984	1988	1992	1996	2000	2004	2008	2012

AFTERNOONS AT THE BEACH

1996 ATLANTA, GEORGIA

Heading into the 1996 Games, the International Olympic Committee (IOC) was excited to see what kind of buzz the new Olympic sport of beach volleyball would generate. Adding beach volleyball as an official event had seemed like a great idea, owing to its rising popularity in the U.S.,

The soft sand of beach volleyball adds to the game's excitement by permitting more dramatic dives and digs

which would be host to the 1996 Olympiad. But trouble arose before the tournament when three associations—the FIVB, the Association of Volleyball Professionals (AVP), and the Women's Volleyball Professional Association (WVPA)—all claimed to run the sport. Finally, the IOC recognized the FIVB as the sport's official governing body, and the tournament's format, rules, and location were able to be finalized.

The first Olympic beach volleyball tournament was played at a specially made venue called Atlanta Beach in Jonesboro, Georgia, 20 miles south of the Olympic Stadium in Atlanta. Sand was trucked in, and seats were erected for 10,000 spectators. Twenty-one countries were represented by a total of 42 teams (24 men's and 18 women's) in the tournament: Argentina, Australia, Brazil, Canada, Cuba, the Czech Republic, Estonia, France, Germany, Great Britain, Indonesia, Italy, Japan, Mexico, the Netherlands, New Zealand, Norway, Portugal, Spain, Sweden, and the U.S. Rules differed from indoor volleyball in that teams consisted of just two players per side rather than the usual six, and matches in the preliminary rounds would be decided in a single set, with the first team to score 15 points declared the victor. The final two medal matches would be played in a best-of-three format, with the first two sets going up to 21 and the third—if needed—going to 15. The tournament would last just six days, a relatively short period that promised a lot of action.

In terms of ticket sellouts, beach volleyball proved to be the third-most popular event at the 1996 Olympics, and the July weather was hot but fine for play. The tournament attracted considerable fan and media attention due to its newness. The event drew attention, too, because some spectators saw it as a "sexy" sport, with participants competing in swimwear. "If people want to come check us out because they're scoping our bodies, I don't have a problem with

Brazil's Sandra Pires was half of the Olympics' first women's beach volleyball championship team

that," said Holly McPeak, an American member of one of the top women's teams, "because I guarantee they'll go home talking about our athleticism."

The inaugural beach volleyball tournament received a boost, too, from the fact that some of the players had previously earned star status in Olympic indoor volleyball. One of the tournament's most intense matches was played between former teammates on gold-medal-winning 1984 and 1988 U.S. men's

volleyball teams when Karch Kiraly and Kent Steffes downed Carl Henkel and Sinjin Smith. Kiraly and Steffes went on to take the gold over another American duo, Mike Dodd and Mike Whitmarsh, while Canadians John Child and Mark Heese captured bronze. On the women's side, Jackie Silva and Sandra Pires defeated Monica Rodrigues and Adriana Samuel in an all-Brazilian finale, while Natalie Cook and Kerri-Ann Pottharst of Australia won the bronze.

The Brazilian women proved their mastery in the sand in 1996, leaving Atlanta with gold and silver

ATHENS, GREECE — 1896
PARIS, FRANCE — 1900
ST. LOUIS, MISSOURI — 1904
LONDON, ENGLAND — 1908
STOCKHOLM, SWEDEN — 1912
ANTWERP, BELGIUM — 1920
PARIS, FRANCE — 1924
AMSTERDAM, NETHERLANDS — 1928
LOS ANGELES, CALIFORNIA — 1932
BERLIN, GERMANY — 1936
LONDON, ENGLAND — 1948
HELSINKI, FINLAND — 1952
MELBOURNE, AUSTRALIA — 1956
ROME, ITALY — 1960
TOKYO, JAPAN — 1964
MEXICO CITY, MEXICO — 1968
MUNICH, WEST GERMANY — 1972
MONTREAL, QUEBEC — 1976
MOSCOW, SOVIET UNION — 1980
LOS ANGELES, CALIFORNIA — 1984
SEOUL, SOUTH KOREA — 1988
BARCELONA, SPAIN — 1992
ATLANTA, GEORGIA — 1996
SYDNEY, AUSTRALIA — 2000
ATHENS, GREECE — 2004
BEIJING, CHINA — 2008
LONDON, ENGLAND — 2012

MISTY WITH A CHANCE OF SUNSHINE

MISTY MAY-TREANOR AND KERRI WALSH U.S. OLYMPIC COMPETITIONS: 2004, 2008

The weather for beach volleyball at the 2008 Olympics in Beijing, China, was not ideal. While many of the other Olympic competitions—such as basketball, swimming, and team volleyball—were held indoors, the beach volleyball competition was held outdoors under the hot China sun and, at times, smog. American duo Misty May-Treanor and Kerri Walsh, the defending gold medalists in women's competition, also found themselves facing a driving rainstorm in the tournament's finale against

Opponents in college, Kerri Walsh (left) and Misty May-Treanor (right) became a dynamic Olympic duo

the Chinese tandem of Tian Jia and Wang Jie. Although the Chinese team fought admirably, May-Treanor and Walsh prevailed in straight sets, 21 – 18, 21 – 18. "The rain made it better," Walsh said afterwards. "I don't know why, but it made it better. We felt like warriors out there."

May-Treanor and Walsh's victory was their 108th straight win, having gone undefeated playing pro beach volleyball after the 2004 Olympics in Athens, Greece—which they competed in and waltzed through without losing a single set to capture gold. In 2008 in Beijing, May-Treanor and Walsh were considered heavy favorites, but the pressure of expectations, the extreme weather, and an increasingly competitive field made their accomplishment even sweeter. "Coming into the Games," said May-Treanor, "I didn't know if winning would feel the same emotionally as last time, but I think it surpassed the medal in Athens because Kerri and I want to start a new chapter in our lives off the court."

What May-Treanor was referring to was the desire both women had to raise families. Both were in their early 30s when the Olympics ended in 2008. Both had grown up in California, even playing against each other in high school and college. In 2000, Walsh was playing indoor volleyball and

competing with the U.S. Olympic team that finished fourth in Sydney, while May-Treanor (known by her maiden name of "May" then, as she had yet to marry her husband, pro baseball catcher Matt Treanor) was competing with Holly McPeak in the Olympic beach volleyball competition, finishing fifth. Walsh and May-Treanor first teamed up in beach volleyball competition in 2001, and after a year of adjusting to each other's styles, they started dominating the sand. The 5-foot-9 May-Treanor had a baffling serve and was adept at all phases of the game but especially excelled at digging and setting. This complemented the 6-foot-3 Walsh's high-jumping, ball-smashing game perfectly. Even their personalities—May-Treanor was quiet and intense, while Walsh had earned the nickname "Six Feet of Sunshine" due to her cheerful disposition— seemed perfectly balanced.

In 2009 and 2010, Walsh gave birth to sons Joseph and Sundance. As of 2011, May-Treanor had yet to experience motherhood. Following their success in Athens and Beijing, many fans were curious about the possibility of the dynamic duo teaming up for London's 2012 Olympiad. "My hope and plan is for Misty and I to get back together and be better than ever," said Walsh. "The goal is to play together and win in 2012."

Walsh and May-Treanor made the capture of gold in 2004 and 2008 look easy, not losing a single set

ATHENS, GREECE | PARIS, FRANCE | ST. LOUIS, MISSOURI | LONDON, ENGLAND | STOCKHOLM, SWEDEN | ANTWERP, BELGIUM | PARIS, FRANCE | AMSTERDAM, NETHERLANDS | LOS ANGELES, CALIFORNIA | BERLIN, GERMANY | LONDON, ENGLAND | HELSINKI, FINLAND | MELBOURNE, AUSTRALIA | ROME, ITALY | TOKYO, JAPAN | MEXICO CITY, MEXICO | MUNICH, WEST GERMANY | MONTREAL, QUEBEC | MOSCOW, SOVIET UNION | LOS ANGELES, CALIFORNIA | SEOUL, SOUTH KOREA | BARCELONA, SPAIN | ATLANTA, GEORGIA | SYDNEY, AUSTRALIA | ATHENS, GREECE | BEIJING, CHINA | LONDON, ENGLAND

1896 | 1900 | 1904 | 1908 | 1912 | 1920 | 1924 | 1928 | 1932 | 1936 | 1948 | 1952 | 1956 | 1960 | 1964 | 1968 | 1972 | 1976 | 1980 | **1984** | 1988 | 1992 | **1996** | 2000 | 2004 | **2008** | 2012

MADE IN CHINA

"JENNY" LANG PING CHINA, U.S. OLYMPIC COMPETITIONS: 1984 (AS CHINESE PLAYER),
1996 (AS CHINESE COACH), 2008 (AS U.S. COACH)

As a 23-year-old in 1984, "Jenny" Lang Ping, a 6-foot-2 outside hitter nicknamed "The Iron Hammer," led the Chinese women's volleyball team to the Olympic gold medal. It was the first medal of any color that China had ever won in Olympic volleyball competition, and it was one of

"Jenny" Lang Ping (left, in action in 1984) moved to the U.S. in 1987 but remained a Chinese citizen

the first medals China had won in any Olympic team sport. As a result of her prowess and success on the court, Lang became a beloved figure in her homeland. She was featured on a postage stamp, sports venues were named in her honor, and her 1987 wedding was broadcast on national TV.

China did not medal in Olympic volleyball again until 1996, when Lang led the Chinese women's team—this time as head coach—to a silver-medal finish. Two years later, Lang gave up the role of coach of the national team in China to try her hand at coaching in the Italian pro leagues. She experienced some success there, but then she also gave that up to move to the U.S., where her daughter Lydia was growing up with her ex-husband, whom she had divorced in 1995.

In 2005, Lang was offered the position of head coach of the U.S. women's national team. It was a tough decision, especially because the Olympics were to be held in China for the first time ever in 2008. Lang wasn't sure how the Chinese people would react, especially if China were to meet the U.S. on the court and Lang was roaming the American sideline, coaching against her homeland. "I waited to see what was happening in China," said Lang. "If there were too many people against this

decision I probably wouldn't have accepted the job. I didn't want to give myself too much trouble." Eventually, Lang made her decision, which was to coach the Americans.

Sure enough, when the 2008 Olympics in Beijing rolled around, the U.S. met China in the fourth match of group competition. The event was turned into a near circus by the Chinese media, and even Chinese president Hu Jintao attended, a rare appearance for the country's leader at the 2008 Games. The match was a thriller, with Lang and the Americans winning in five sets, 23–25, 25–22, 23–25, 25–20, and 15–11. Afterward, Lang tried to downplay the Americans' victory. "I tried to be very concentrated on the game, not to be more emotionally involved," she said. "I feel very proud because it shows that Chinese volleyball is respected. That's why the Americans hired me. This is a proud moment for China."

The U.S. and China nearly met again in the gold-medal match, but China was beaten in the semifinals by Brazil after the U.S. upset Cuba. China beat Cuba to win the bronze medal—its first since Lang had coached them to silver in 1996—and the U.S. team lost to Brazil to take silver, its first medal since 1992.

ATHENS, GREECE 1896
PARIS, FRANCE 1900
ST. LOUIS, MISSOURI 1904
LONDON, ENGLAND 1908
STOCKHOLM, SWEDEN 1912
ANTWERP, BELGIUM 1920
PARIS, FRANCE 1924
AMSTERDAM, NETHERLANDS 1928
LOS ANGELES, CALIFORNIA 1932
BERLIN, GERMANY 1936
LONDON, ENGLAND 1948
HELSINKI, FINLAND 1952
MELBOURNE, AUSTRALIA 1956
ROME, ITALY 1960
TOKYO, JAPAN 1964
MEXICO CITY, MEXICO 1968
MUNICH, WEST GERMANY 1972
MONTREAL, QUEBEC 1976
MOSCOW, SOVIET UNION 1980
LOS ANGELES, CALIFORNIA 1984
SEOUL, SOUTH KOREA 1988
BARCELONA, SPAIN 1992
ATLANTA, GEORGIA 1996
SYDNEY, AUSTRALIA 2000
ATHENS, GREECE 2004
BEIJING, CHINA 2008
LONDON, ENGLAND 2012

THE GAMES OF 2012

The 2012 Olympics were to be held in London, England. Londoners got the news in July 2005, and as is the case any time an Olympic host is selected, city and national officials sprang into action. Although seven years may seem to be plenty of time for preparation, it is in fact a small window when one considers that host cities typically need to create housing for thousands of

In 2012, London was to play host to its third Summer Olympiad, having done so in 1908 and 1948

international athletes and coaches (generally in a consolidated area known as the "Athletes' Village"), expand public transportation options (such as trains and buses), and build outdoor playing fields, indoor arenas, and other venues with enough seating—and grandeur—to be worthy of Olympic competition.

The numbers involved in the 2012 Games indicate just how large a venture it is to host an Olympiad. Some 10,500 athletes from 200 countries were to compete in London, with 2,100 medals awarded. About 8 million tickets were expected to be sold for the Games. And before any athletes arrived or any medals were awarded, it was anticipated that the total cost of London's Olympics-related building projects and other preparations would approach $15 billion.

Among those construction projects was the creation of Olympic Park, a sprawling gathering area in east London that was to function as a center of activity during the Games. From the park, people would be able to move to numerous athletic facilities in and around the city. Those facilities included the 80,000-seat Olympic Stadium, which was built to host track

and field events as well as the opening and closing ceremonies; the new Basketball Arena, a temporary structure that was to be dismantled after the Games; and the $442-million Aquatics Centre, which was designed both to host swimming events and to serve as a kind of visitors' gateway to Olympic Park. Other notable venues included the North Greenwich Arena (which was to host gymnastics), the ExCeL center (boxing), Earls Court (indoor volleyball), and Horse Guards Parade (beach volleyball).

In July 2011, British prime minister David Cameron and IOC president Jacques Rogge reviewed all preparations and proudly declared that the city was nearly ready to welcome the world. "This has the makings of a great British success story," Cameron announced. "With a year to go, it's on time, it's on budget.... We must offer the greatest ever Games in the world's greatest country."

Rogge kicked off the one-year countdown to the Games by formally inviting countries around the world to send their greatest athletes to the British capital in 2012. "The athletes will be ready," said Rogge. "And so will London."

bloc — a group (of countries, for example) that is united for a common cause or action

blocker — a volleyball player who attempts to stop the opposing team's hits, especially spikes, from crossing the net

boycotts — acts of protesting or showing disapproval of something by refusing to participate in an event

bumps — hits a volleyball, usually when receiving a serve or spike from the opposing team; a team is allowed three hits in succession, and a bump is usually first, followed by a set and then a spike

communist — describing a government that has tight control over a country's resources and people; many communist countries were rivals of the U.S. from the late 1940s to the early 1990s

democratic — describing a government in which leaders are elected by the people and that affords its citizens great individual freedoms

dig — to hit or redirect a spiked ball, using the forearms, just before it makes contact with the ground

dumps — volleyball plays in which the ball is tapped lightly over the net in attempts to catch the opposing team off-guard or out of position

dynasty — a team, family, or group that maintains power or dominance over a long period of time

hitter — a volleyball player who receives a set and then swings his or her arm at the ball with great force to attempt a kill; a hitter may also be called a spiker

kill — to end a rally (the back-and-forth volley that determines one point) by grounding the volleyball in the opposing team's court or hitting it off an opposing player without the possibility of a return

knockout round — the round of a tournament in which a loss immediately eliminates a team

match point — the point that clinches victory for a team and ends the match; match point varies according to which set it is and whether the format is indoor or beach volleyball, but a team must win with at least a two-point advantage

pool play — a tournament format in which all athletes or teams play each other at least once, and failure to win a contest does not result in immediate elimination

preliminary — leading up to the main event; preliminary events serve to narrow a field of athletes to only the best competitors

round-robin — describing a style of tournament in which each team plays every other team in its assigned group, and only the team or teams with the best record advance to the next stage

serve — to hit the volleyball from the back boundary line of the court across the net to begin a rally or "volley"

sets — in volleyball, the games that make up a match; in Olympic indoor volleyball today, a set goes up to 25 points (15 in the case of a fifth set), and a match is won by whichever team wins 3 sets first

setter — a volleyball player who, using a two-handed, over-the-head pushing motion, lofts the ball high to set up a hitter for the spike; a team's setter is usually responsible for calling out plays or strategy for teammates to follow

shantytowns — towns or sections of towns in which poor people live in crudely built huts or shacks

slums — run-down and usually heavily populated urban areas

spike — to jump up, usually close to the net, and hit the ball into the opponent's court, usually at great speed and a sharp downward angle

steroids — chemical substances or drugs that affect muscle growth; some athletes have used them illegally to become stronger and faster

Selected Bibliography

Anderson, Dave. *The Story of the Olympics*. New York: HarperCollins, 2000.

Farber, Michael. "Fun in the Sun." *Sports Illustrated*, August 5, 1996.

Guttmann, Allen. *The Olympics: A History of the Modern Games*. Urbana: University of Illinois Press, 2002.

Jares, Joe. "The Sole Pole for the Sol." *Sports Illustrated*, August 22, 1977.

MacCambridge, Michael, ed. *SportsCentury*. New York: ESPN, 1999.

Macy, Sue, and Bob Costas. *Swifter, Higher, Stronger: A Photographic History of the Summer Olympics*. Washington, D.C.: National Geographic, 2008.

Osborne, Mary Pope. *Ancient Greece and the Olympics*. New York: Random House, 2004.

Whitehead, Eric. "Driven Beyond Dignity." *Sports Illustrated*, March 16, 1964.

Web Sites

International Olympic Committee
www.olympic.org
This site is the official online home of the Olympics and features profiles of athletes, overviews of every sport, coverage of preparation for the 2012 Summer Games, and more.

Sports-Reference / Olympic Sports
www.sports-reference.com/olympics
This site is a comprehensive database for Olympic sports and features complete facts and statistics from all Olympic Games, including medal counts, Olympic records, and more.

INDEX

Published by Creative Education
P.O. Box 227, Mankato, Minnesota 56002
Creative Education is an imprint of
The Creative Company
www.thecreativecompany.us

Design and production by The Design Lab
Art direction by Rita Marshall

Printed by Corporate Graphics in
the United States of America

Photographs by Alamy (ACE STOCK LIMITED, Everett Collection Inc, Igor Golovnov), American Numismatic Society, Dreamstime (Alain Lacroix), Corbis (Giuliano Bevilacqua/Sygma, Leo Mason, Franck Seguin/TempSport), Getty Images (Scott Barbour/ALLSPORT, Larry Burrows/Time Life Pictures, Getty Images, Richard Mackson/Sports Illustrated, Doug Pensinger, AIZAR RALDES/AFP, JOEL ROBINE/AFP, Sankei Archive, Jamie Squire, Bob Thomas, TORU YAMANAKA/AFP), iStockphoto (ray roper), Shutterstock (Antonio Abrignani, Andre Nantel, rook76)

Library of Congress
Cataloging-in-Publication Data
LeBoutillier, Nate.
Volleyball / by Nate LeBoutillier.
p. cm. — (Summer Olympic legends)
Includes bibliographical references and index.
Summary: A survey of the highlights and legendary athletes—such as Soviet Yuri Chesnokov—of the Olympic sport of volleyball, which officially became a part of the modern Summer Games in 1964.
ISBN 978-1-60818-213-8
1. Volleyball players—Biography—Juvenile literature. 2. Volleyball—Juvenile literature. 3. Olympics—Juvenile literature. I. Title.
GV1015.25.L43 2012
796.325—dc23   2011032499

CPSIA: 070212 PO1591

9 8 7 6 5 4 3 2